The Estate

SASHA DUGDALE was born in Sussex. Between 1995 and 2000 she lived and worked in Russia. In 1999 she initiated the Russian theatre New Writing project with the Royal Court theatre, London, for whom she has translated numerous Russian plays. Her translation of *Plasticine* by Vassily Sigarev won the *Evening Standard* Award for Most Promising Playwright in 2002, and in 2004 she won a translation prize from the Stephen Spender Trust for her translations of poems by Elena Shvarts. Her translations of the Russian poet Tatiana Shcherbina, *Life Without*, are published by Bloodaxe. Her first, *Notebook*, was published by Carcanet/OxfordPoets.

T0148925

Also by Sasha Dugdale from Carcanet Oxford*Poets*

Notebook

SASHA DUGDALE

The Estate

Oxford*Poets*

CARCANET

Acknowledgements

Poems from *The Estate* have been published in *Modern Poetry in Translation*, *Poetry Wales*, *The Wolf* and *PN Review*. The translations of Akhmatova were commissioned by Ruth Borthwick for the Poetry International Festival in 2005. 'Island' was commissioned by the MLA South East.

I would like to thank the British Council, Russia and most of all Anna Genina, who introduced me to Mikhailovskoye and supported my visits there. I am also grateful to the Estate Museum, and particularly to its director Georgiy Vassilevich and to Konstantin and Rimma Burchenkov, for their hospitality during my visits.

First published in Great Britain in 2007 by
Carcanet Press Limited
Alliance House
Cross Street
Manchester M2 7AQ

A CIP catalogue record for this book is available from the British Library
ISBN 978 1 903039 80 9

The publisher acknowledges financial assistance from Arts Council England

Typeset by XL Publishing Services, Tiverton
Printed and bound in England by SRP Ltd, Exeter

Contents

The Estate

There is a popular legend that Pushkin set out to see his friends in St Petersburg from Mikhailovskoye, his family's estate, in the winter of 1825. A hare ran across his path and Pushkin turned back, thinking this to be a bad sign. A few days later his friends took part in the Decembrist uprising and were executed or sentenced to exile and hard labour.

The following eleven poems were written at Mikhailovskoye.

Zayats is the Russian for hare; ozero is the Russian for lake.

Zayats

Noon, and the woods are still bright
With the sun, the snow that fell last night.
The birds, the few that haven't gone
Are watched by a fisherman, crouching alone.
I've been here a while by the lake
Where the ice is marbled, opaque
I've been here a while, sniffing about
Wondering if he will come riding out
Knowing that he must come riding by
Past the dark mill on the rise
As he approaches through the snow
I will prick my ears and I will know
And then when he draws close at last
I will throw myself across his path.

The Hare

The way it leapt along
As if the ground was several miles below
As if it grasped the air in every paw
Arrowing its way across the forest floor
Towards us over the melting snow.

My horse was fast and strong
But at this creature's sudden flight
It stopped and swayed and pawed the slippy track
And showed its teeth and stepped back
Slid and recovered itself in its great fright.

There is nothing wrong
Still I turn the horse into a cloud of our breath.
I will not pass through its little prints –
I cannot cross this line: and since
I cannot, there may be hope yet.

Hare's Breadth

Points like this in everyone's life.
Metaphorical hares, virtual black cats,
Lines you have promised yourself
Not to cross, thin walls like unseen glass
Bloodying your heart, time and time again.

If you did so you would be lost.
It would work a hole in you, the grain
Would seep through onto the stone floor
And soon you would be all holes, good
For nothing. Empty as the day you were born.

He turned back. It is a legend, not the truth
But living so by myth, by myth we die.
And then the news – his friends are gone:
Buried and scattered, every last one,
And he on his way to them.

The weather turns and comes in low
Above the little house and tree-lined yard.
For months the snow is piled around the door
For months he lies in bed and writes and writes
Cursed by self-pity and the failing light.

And all of real life out there.
Beyond the white snow, the horizon, the hare
And the honour that he covets, offending soul
He can only give his pen and paper for
Drawing pin-men on a gallows of dark ink.

We must do what we must do.
A woman tells him this to comfort him
They will uncover the billiard table, find the cues,
The river will soon melt, it is spring
And the hare at least is his. The ice stirs.

The Rope

Yes, I admit I thought of it –
The lake down there, the river,
The splintering ice.
The pair of guns on the wall
Pointing respectfully up to the sky.
But I wrote and what I wrote
Was a rope.

As a child you often play the game –
Lying still on an old divan
Daisies, roses.
But this was murderous and cold
Wading with rocks in my trousers.
Still I wrote. And I wrote my
Own rope.

Every scratch, every blot and curl
Jottings, drawings. All of it
Attempts at a life.
I made a cell for him in a poem
That little man who walked on ice
And when I wrote, I wrote him
A rope.

The Footstool

*There is an avenue of trees named the Kern-allee, after Anna Kern,
to whom Pushkin dedicated a love poem. A footstool in the Pushkin house
is said to belong to her.*

Now she lives on in a worn footstool
And a long alley of trees. Back then
He was in love and he was a fool.
Love should be tragic, she, desperate, invents
Love now and tragic later, he is firm
And seals her mouth with a poem
A good one, an argument for sperm
And she is persuaded to find his seed a home –
The sapling poem rooted in her womb.
For later generations to wander in.

And so he has his love, and now she sees
It is the only thing she is remembered for.
The alley where they kissed between the trees
The footstool he knelt on when she said no more.

The Myth Maker

Sleep, child, and I will tell you a tale
Of a myth maker who lives near here.
Often before dawn he rises from bed
And bathes in the lake where the fishes swim.
And then walks out, with his berry and thread
And all the women rush to see him.

No one is indifferent, not the fat cook
Who tucks a red lock behind her ear
And rolls the pastry dangerous thin
And pretends she doesn't see him there
Teasing an apple with his teeth at the door.
She rolls on and her face is marvellous soft.

Nor the big ladies, each one in love
With his ugly face and his slenderest waist.
He is not entirely of this world, that's why –
He is made of a pattern of stories, that's why –
He takes them all and in return he gives
A piece of his myth to make them rich.

Dangerous, why? Because he will see them fly
The lonely, ungainly, the heartworn and heavy.
And they do fly briefly, but see their faces beneath them
In the river's black, and find themselves women
Not birds or fish, and fall like stars into bushes
And their husbands find them all scratchy with briars.

Fight him? Oh fight him with not believing
And at first he will make you a castle of stories
And life ever after, and still you walk from him.
Then the walls of his castle fall down,
And he is angry and hurt and he fights like a child –
And again you are his as you rush to console him.

Love him? Yes, but I will not be with him –
There is room for just one in his endless mything
And I will not be his fish, nor watch him fishing
His golden fish to grant all his wishes
His golden wish to rest from his fishes
I am busy at home making myths of my own.

The Room

There were times when alone I willed you to appear
I wanted so hard I felt the papered walls sway.
I became for that time minutely aware
And every tremble and whisper oppressed my ear.
Every pattern on the quilt became two, then four
The room teemed with patterns and I was only one
Then all the bright words that I thought were gone
Came back and blinded me and I was sore
Till I spoke them and gave them air to breathe
Just as, it seems, you like to think you've done
With me, your single word, breathing on my own
And every breath a cry because you leave and leave
But it passes. It passes and you relent
And rush to find me, love, when all my own is spent.

From the Window

Stand with me here to watch the woman entering
With the pails in her hands spilling slightly on the ground
He stops her. Listen. Listen to this, my darling,
Reads something from a book of philosophy aloud.
At first she's mad with anger. What if, right now
I took a pail in both hands and swung and aimed
At his head, it would break across his brow –
With one blow free of man, and one less pail to drain.
But he reads to her of patience, of swaddling her anger
And standing it outside, under the tree in the sun,
And she listens against her will and then forgetting
She sags against the doorframe and he reads on.
And at the end he fades. Etcetera etcetera
She stirs nodding, rubs her eyes and stands
And then bends for the pails and lifts them both
With the cloths round the handles to protect her hands
And carries them slowly out towards the stove
And warms the pan of food and opens up a can
And takes down a plate and a knife and a glass.

Tonight there is no wind but the door blows open
And outside a hare is sobbing in the grass.

Ozero

We met at the water's edge in winter
And looked down into the calmest black
And I say swim, but he holds back
And takes my wrist in case I swim.
Pity to set such calm astir, he says
But I am bold: where's the pity in that?

It hasn't always been cold, once we swam
And it was silk and sun rode on our backs,
Today the sun touches the trees' white bones.
So pity the water which reflects us black,
In the chill of our hearts, the depth of the
Clouds, the slightness of stars.

The water is as black as the ground, unwavering
Black. He writes to say he won't come back.
The trees are bones and the windows all white
Where I look. There is no day, only night.
A black mass of twigs on the bank, and
The water mouthing a silent song.

The clouds are veined at sunset. The red
Cracks the night and weeps from the cut,
I will dig out a grave with a bone
And an antler, he says. Place you in it myself.
Tend and water the ground till I die.
But I ask you, where's the pity in that?

The Real Gift

It seemed then as if I had the real gift.
He spoke with me. He was working the soil
But he stands the spade against his leg
Lights up. Come close
Let me tell you how I lost my home
After years of bloody airborne.
How I returned.

Do you know about that?
Do you?

For eight years I built. I sawed
And chopped and placed the wood
And made a home around the compass points
Of my heart. Where I could take my fatigue.

And then my nephew took a lighted match
Between his soft fingers to a cigarette
And dropped it. Down under the porch it guttered
And then fate willed it to flare and catch.

My only home.
I didn't beat him. I didn't touch him.
I took a job to pay for wood
And started again. And I am still building. Fate.
Fate wakes me in the morning. Fate sets me down.
Isn't that how it is?

Quiet. A squirrel watches us.
There is a bear
In the woods.
It fears people like fire.

Yes. In your place, years suspended over deserts
Friends lost to the casual deaths
Fate threads to soldiers, one two,
One two
Floating down into the mouths of cannons

My heart would be set on fate and I would not be wanting
To question her indifference.

There was a fire.
The villagers gathered.
Only the bear fled unseen
Like a lover.

And there is the gift.
I am with him, for seconds in his reflection.
I stand beside him and warm him with my breath
He wipes his mouth,
He nods faintly.
He begins working once again.

When I paddled my sled with mittened hand
I was riding across a continent
Dreaming already of a stranger land.

But when I arrived it was hideous and grand,
An adult hell that wasn't meant
To be and shame I hadn't planned.

And my own horror appeared bland
Like twisted flesh after an accident
Warmly familiar, although already unmanned,

And staring shamelessly back, as if it shammed
And infecting me with its intent:
To make the paying audience stand.

So I stood, was adult and damned
The whim that took me when I went –
Dreaming already of a stranger land

And seeing desolation at first hand
Driven on by a child who would not relent
When I paddled my sled with mittened hand
Dreaming already of a stranger land

★

Island

No man is an island. No,
No man could seem this remote
From the near shore of another's reach –
A little grey mound in the big grey sea.

No one person could be this desired
Across the gulf, could contain in their veins
That quiet, or the nervous system of stones
And seasons with the same small time.

No thing could remain so finally other
Though the birds move between, the clouds
Pass over. Might have been Russia or even China
Might have been pack ice, floating, floating

Normandy. August 1944

That soldier has refused all food, sleep.
He sits down there by the water.
Look at the light, hanging over the pool,
Our pool. Look at that light.
He is writing a letter. I hear the scratch of a pen.
Scratch, and a bunch of burnt fingers slide
Along the line.

Now the weather has turned,
Now we are chasing. I walked through fire
To be here, in this light, by this pool –
If only you could see the house martins,
The best sight I saw hereabouts.
Swooping and pulling the insects from the air –
I walked through burning air to see that sight.

They tell me here about a man the Germans took
And threw into a furnace.
What has prepared us for all this?
Where did I read at school that men
Could be dissolved in fire?

All nature is at peace. We are chasing now
The weather has turned. Autumn is not quite here,
But my nerves remember it and draw it out
Of the air towards my fingers.

I wish I could tell you how my mind is,
Empty of ambition, of nostalgia. Nothing left.
Nothing left but the memory of autumn
Growing and blowing, skittering away

The first leaf from a Bayeux beech.

I am in the middle of my life and quite alone –
Unaccompanied by thoughts that go before
And go behind. I have prepared myself for death
Like an old man on a bench, left with the light
Over the pool, the house martins tunnelling
Down the air, the memory of autumn.

He writes and writes. His hands' bandages
Loosen with the writing. My mother says
He has the most wondering eyes she ever saw.
My daughter says he will be moving on soon.

War

This shouting may have lasted weeks.
The two of them, the fearful kitchen light.
The hoarse voices, rigid ligament,
The spots of flush, the blood flowing to the eyes.
And no one remembers how it started anymore
What little lapse of patience gave it form
Because now it is everywhere. Like smoke,
Like the far-off shelling of a town.
Now it is the resentment of a thousand years
The bitterness of kings and queens, the box
Bursting as it lands. It is an old well of hate
They both dip their jugs in and bring up
Time and time again to drink from.
And then she says something so bad it dances from
Her lips and he instinctively lifts his hand to ward it off
And then to hit, and she cowers, fears yet understands
That if he hits her, the pain will harden for all time
Her hate. And he understands
That he must hit, must return this hurt
And hits himself, hard, hard upon his own cheek.
This sacrifice breaks the spell. She stops his hands
And kisses his burning cheek and cries and cries
And they stand there and hold each other, ruined, limp
And against her head he throbs and watches insects high
Under the roof, round and round the bulb they fly.

Pskov Wedding (1941–1944)

How long must I write and love
Before I can tell the tale of Pskov?

Pskov wedding. The guests are sheaves
Around a bride, so artfully decorated
As to make time stand still and the body
Incorruptible.

A trumpet sounded then, and a child,
Stretched over the parallel bars like the skin
Of a drum, upon which the broad onslaught
Of winter rolls,

And all of them seeming to have casts in their eyes,
The blue, unstarred, the blue of night in summertime
And hair so fair it made me stare
At the soldiers on the platform.

I marched alone, the river's triangle, the fisher's ditch,
And on up Gitlerstrasse, whose puddles and furrows
I skipped, I knew no fears against the flanks
And row on row of *men* with *girls* –

And saw the wedding there. Some boy in a tracksuit took me for a
nun
At the monastery. I lay down on the grass and wept for the asters
and dahlias
And my tears were wild and profligate so close to autumn
In a body as white as the walls.

But tell me this. Did anyone weep on the eve of the coming?
Did they love in small rooms around dangerous stoves?
Such beloved, wedded flesh, *Skobari*, weep for it!

Was it the weight of tears, so help me tears,
Forced to the ground, where I lay on my back
And watched the whirring bees?

So winter follows summer, and winter once again,
Careless of what passes as history beneath:

A slight bride, in her own weight of satin and gold
Standing like a spindle between earth and sky
And a photographer who turns, aims through the crowd –

And mocks them gravely,
                      is this a funeral I see?

The Conscript

Last night in the washroom here in the barracks
We took revenge on little Mohammed.
He is an odd arrangement of flesh-and-blood
In the circle's centre when the light goes on.
We were throwing punches, kicks, in the darkness.
Casting our winning hands into the ring –
But silent, because it needed no comment
And Mohammed breathed and was sick without speaking.
In the morning the commander is hard like a stone
And says clean yourself up. It's not good for morale.

But Mohammed sits with one eye on the outside
Whispers through the slit in the face he once owned
I know who you are. I know where you're sleeping
I will come with a knife. I will have revenge.
And we're frightened. Oh Mum. Your own little boy
Slashed in his bunk. How would you live?
And I'm nervous, washing the blood from my fingers
In the bucket of water down by my bed.

The cat we feed with milk from a mess tin
Jumps up on the window, he is empty and spry
With a whole night's mating down in the village
And he sucks up the milk and wanders away.

An Education

'Oh no. They were more formal in my day.
They used to cane the boys. I mean,
Imagine that. No chatting with the teachers.'
And I wonder again at it – the impulse
To beat and pulp the disobedience out
Of a child. And then remember our teacher
Taking the cartoonish bending cane from
Beneath the desk and beckoning to one
Whose lies and snotty nose made him no friend of his
Or ours, and how, quivering, whining like a dog,
The boy went forward, convinced of pain –
Feeling it in his fingers: the precipitous end
To all his parents' rows.
The teacher lifts the cane and frowns
And winks at us, his conspirators, bringing it down
Like thunder on the varnished desk, past the boy's
Frozen face. And says, 'Ye gods and little
Fishes, twenty years ago I'd of had you there for that.'
And we are howling with complicity, squealing
Did you see that there and *oh I could have killed myself.*
And the teacher's only thirty, quite a lad, with a smile
For the bonny lollipop lady on duty after school.

Death of a Cat

It didn't feel like anything more than hitting a rock,
A soft bag flapping on the road. There was no crack
Of bone to ruin the day, no unnatural scream
From the cat's throat. Just the sense of a thing
Rolling between the roundrubber wheels
Between the road and the car's dark axles, gears,
With the frenzy of a ball in a fruit machine
Flipped to and fro until it rolls clean.

It lay twitching and then was still and dead
The side presented to me – whole, the head
A perfect diminutive, the collar and the silver coin
Were normal, everyday – a house number, its name.
But the other half, pressed down against the road
Was quite different: flat and wet with blood
Covering even the wide, malignant eyeball
A butcher's morsel, flayed and growing cold.

The cat's death mask – half-horror, half-demure
Made me think of the fortune teller's booth
On the front, where the gypsy's plastic face
Is Sindy-pretty from the side, but otherwise a mess:
One black Cassandra eye gouged out with little skill
Above the rosebud mouth – a sudden view of hell.
Until you pay her she looks silently out to sea
And watches waves reclaim the sagging pier.

The blood spreads inch by inch around the corpse
In a lake of some unnatural brilliant juice,
And beyond the concentrated violence of the spot
A verge of daffodils, a wilting clump of snowdrops
Further down a crocus patch, fields, and beyond that
A glittering sea and across it a sun track.
But when I stand, bloodrush, a glance to the sky
I see: nothing. Nothing. Then a magpie.

Spain

In Spain there were many new kinds of birds,
Ones he did not know, in the moist
Foliage at noon, at dusk spots on the shore.
He pushed me against a cactus twice.
Extracted the long spines from my skull.
He tells me we are fighting a war.
He writes all night, steals the words
From the Fascists. Then we shout
About freedom. He calls me a whore
When I say Franco will outlive us all.
But it is he who gives in, it is he who falls
And lies there wet and whispers and stirs
And moans about the tombs behind glass in a wall
And the hasty shovelling of bodies he saw
And fears burial alive under a Catholic pall.
Go home, I say. I hold some ice
To his head, and pray for his soul.
Go home. He is sick with the war
And now he is mortal and hurting and poor,
And I watch him leave. He is gone like a bird.

Cypresses

The cypresses on the hillside were distinct
On the first evening: dark figures
Caught after a rainstorm in the last
Cold sunlight. Stiff, slightly numb,
The light fading, we tried the electricity
And in desperation lit a fire
Of brushwood, long flaming feathery branches
Overlaid with the cypress logs.
It was very warm. Too warm by the fire
And too cold elsewhere. We watched
It taking: settled our eyes on its formlessness
And someone said, 'Those trees are Phaeton's sisters.
Weeping at his body consumed by fire, and pliant,
Bending branches in their supple grief
Because Phaeton wrestled with his father's sun
And died.' But his sisters loved him.
They mourn up there on the hills
As no one in the West mourns the young dead
With the hysteric ritual of grief, from which
We hide our eyes, cast them elsewhere.
Nothing much remained of the young man:
A gold button, maybe, a few hairs coming to rest
On the sands, the debris of the chariot scattered
Over many many miles. It was an act of mercy
To change them into trees and release them from
Their human grief. Sometimes it is better to be wood,
And wear the attitude of mourning numbly.

The Casting

I could not sit alone in a house of our making.
That was my dream – the door swinging ajar
And signs of a last meal and a fire – finished.
The ashes and the single remaining charred branch.

And all that afternoon I heard birds singing.
On the windows a sparrow or two, the starling
The one you called greedy, was a bird today, no more.

The blacked grate reflected no loving
The lintels over the doors were heavy
And the small light disappeared from the front window first –

And yet, if I heard you coming, how I would rush
To make a fire and how I would take burning sticks
And light each lamp until our small place
Was as loud and warm as a firebox

And you would emerge from the smoke
And I would crouch in the foreground with oranges
And open each one in turn until the pulp lay deep
Over the slates and I would tie a coloured star to the beam

And lace the cot sheets with magpie-blue –
But where is the enterprise in dreaming so?

He will not have me as his friend
He houses our love where I cannot go.

One of those

It was one of those days: two boys
Travelling home on the train after work
And one says see this chain – I got it
Down at the market, cheap as dirt. Solid,
Carat gold, just like a snake. The scaly band
Slips from his neck and round his arm.
And the other says one of these days.
One of these days I'll buy the same
And he reaches out a moist and hungry hand,

Receives the gold and holds it jealous
At his throat. See, right there his skin is soft
And the man sitting by them turns to stare.
He looks: he looks too long and looks too much,
Till snap, the chain is clasped back in its place
And the man quickly turns to look elsewhere.

And in him, on that day, one of those
Trips he made in childhood to the zoo
Surfaces and as clear as day
He sees again the python in its case
Its muscles slipping under scales
Ceramic, like the glaze on chemists' bowls,
How it snapped its mouth round little eggs
Beyond the reflection of his face
But otherwise lay blank and overcoiled –

It is one of those days. Today this man
Will run a bath and let it run and run, whilst the boys
Will pass the chain between them, back and forth –
A blank repetition of their love
Born of boredom, born of days
Like these between the job the train the pub.

The Roof of the Dome

Pelican, letting your children peck
Your lifeblood, all your bodily organs
From your breast – you are the guarantor
Of life after death. For any torment
Such as this must be rewarded
Somewhere, must it not?
And surely in some other place
The fires are stoked, the knives are sharpened
For the tenderloving flaying
Of the intact beasts of earth?

The New Achilles

I am the new Achilles; I keep my watch in my pocket
And I circle the sawdust with the blood on my thigh.
I see nothing but the feathers from the fighting birds
I hear nothing but the fighting birds' cry.

I place my trust in God; keep the virgin on my side
In a column of blue robes she sways against the ropes
Which have his blood on them, deep in the fibres
His blood which I let in return for my own.

His hands I kiss: they make niches over my body
One for each saint's day I honour with my heart.
My hands take his flesh and dispose of it lightly
My hands take his fleece and tear it apart.

When they tear us apart my spirit ups and leaves me
My eyes glisten moist in a mirror of a gaze –
They sluice me with water, press ice to my temples
Say nothing of the death in this darkening face.

But a camera flashes. I keep the photo by me
When I wander in this town where I used to be known.
Oh I would rather be the cheapest cockfighter
Than see myself still alive, but empty and gone.

Dido

It is 7.10. The boat has left.
She knows. She knew all along
And now she sits and files her nails
At a café table and sings fever.

She has told the nanny to stay late
She sits and files. It is 7.12
The boat is still visible. She knew
All along. *Never knew how much...*

She will have perfect nails.
Her last lullaby is sung and
The boat is dwindling but not yet gone.
It is 7.15. Some wine

She sings, now her mind is made up
She is quite undone. Filing fast
She sings *Lord you got me*
Over and over. The night comes.

The boat is a speck. It is 7.
20 and darkness everywhere
She must slip into something finer
She knew. Oh she knew all along.

7.30. She lays her ten fingers
On the table and compares each one.
There is a begging child. She gives it
Money, shakes the varnish, brushes on

Vermeil, flawless like her clothes.
Dark as the streets, her dress and
Darker still her nails, the boat
Is all gone and now she knows

Fever! she sings again, it is a
Looping song, too late to stop
Singing it will soon be 8
It will soon be over, she knew

All along, she sings fever and
Blows her drying fingers, blows
Kisses into the sky and sings
More wine for Dido. She is all sung.

Jealous Painter

after Gwen John

Loosening the black gloves as if her fingers
Were china, she sits in the front room
Looking around her. Playing for time
I stand and observe her, my model. No less
Do I hate her for this preciousness.
The tilt of her head, her Christian head
All dolorous, righteous before she comes to bed.

And comes from it, cunt smells of pilchard,
She will not do nude but her clothes cannot hide it
And the cord that she wears at the nape of her neck
Bears the ugliest cross and a martyr outstretched.
And the eyes I can't bear, for their vaults of black
Like an unlit cathedral or an untied sack.
I tug at my brooch with shaking fingers.

It's you, she exclaims, in feigned delight
For she must have seen my shadow before
And she gathers her bags and moves to the door.
I should stop and say, I have made a mistake
But instead I say sorry for making her wait.
I take a brush and I clean it with the force of pure hate
Then I start and she poses like a pious saint.

With my brush I undress her. Every pin and clasp
I undo and display the flesh in the glass
The thin little carcass, I lay her quite bare
Nothing to hide her, but the cross and the hair
And the sharp little tits and the ugly skin
And the outer expression and what lies within
At cross purposes. I have won. Never lie to me again.

Commonplace

We went shopping. He pushed the trolley
And people we knew saw us and smiled.
That afternoon he worked, walked with me,
Played a few tunes on the piano, admired
A thriving plant, warm against the house,
A postcard, the grate's neat fire.

And then bed, earlier than he was used to go.
And once he called me and asked if I was there.
So I went up, undressed and unpinned my hair
And lay beside him in his own halo.

Nothing. Then later a movement in the air
And from a deep scared dream I woke,
He sighed quietly, touched me and spoke
Of his love. And then he was no longer there.

Left

after Akhmatova

Night after night. Night
After night I lay there in the room
Where once on a folding table
We ate oysters off a bed of bladderwrack
On a tin platter. Now the room is bare –
Not even the tattered remains of curtains
To stretch with one trembling hand across
My bareness. This pain, the pain of waiting
In vain, of lying here stinking under
Bald fur coats, without perfume, or silk
Or lipstick. Distilled woman. Gutted
Like the last day's catch and splayed on the bed.
Roaring like a teeming beast. I do not know this voice
It comes from some bloody abyss within,
Frightens me as much as the other waiting women.
Who would want this much? Not you
Whose departing back gleamed with buttons.
But once, when I shoved a hand into an unyielding sleeve
And tugged, the white roses came tumbling one after the other,
Rose after rose, rose after rose, and you turned on me and said,
You must never go.

Three Adaptations of Poems by Anna Akhmatova

1

The purple marks he left
Have faded from my mind, the visions
In my head. There is a sea mist
Today, and the shadows of birds
On the water.

I can hear the shrill gannets
From the stacks, their ancient shapes
Hidden in the fog. The fulmars
Stand in the air close to us and call.

I was picking faded flowers on the cliffs –
Seapink and tiny spring squill.
Just now two puffins landed on the grass
With fish-filled beaks, and scuttled past.

I want it back, the real world,
To touch and grasp, blinded as I am –
Still I am healed, I have been cured
With departed love's icy calm.

2

Everything – taken, betrayed, traded,
Death's crow's-wing has flashed through the sky
We are skin and bones with the hunger of yearning –
Then suddenly, suddenly this light.

Day breathes cherry blossom through the leaves
Of a magical forest beyond city walls
The furthest corners of sheer July nights
Are reached for and touched by new stars.

And the miracle passes within a hair's breadth
Of our crumbling, blackened homes
None of us, none of us see it
But we've longed for it all of our lives.

3

I remember your words
As if from the edge of a cloud,

And with my words your nights
Became as bright as days.

We were torn from the earth
And soared as high as stars

Beyond despair and shame,
What is, what will be and was,

But as you live and wake
You hear me calling out.

And the door you left ajar
I don't have the strength to close.

Poet

Her work is influenced by folk music from her native region.
Her work is influenced by village women singing,
Or giving birth, crouching in the pastures.
Her work is influenced by peasant costume
The embroidered jerkins and the lace.
Her work smells of the fresh mountain air
And the vast plain. The endless land
And the sudden sea. Her work is full
Of allusions to the homeland. A native language
Oppressed, but now reviving
Around the hearths of native homes.
Her work is born of the local storyteller
Weaving magic from the bench outside her hut.
Her work is born of the men who sit in silence
And the century of grime which lines their hands.
Her work is full of the earth's demanding,
She gathers it from every village tree,
Sees a woman standing beneath them with an apple.

A glass apple, ornate and pointless.
A glass apple, a table decoration.

And she says, you can't eat it,
That apple.
It's glass.

And the woman looks. She looks in her direction
Mutters with what was once a mouth

Who on earth do you take me for?

Apple

The apple that you gave me:
Kissed and blushing. Mute
And secret as the very heart
Itself, pulsing away in my bag
With a sound like crumpling paper
In each contraction. It was bruised
Upon arrival and eating around the bruise
Was hell on the street. So I threw it
Into a smoking bin – Black urn in the snow
Take my suffering love – I have no need
For mute, secret suffering.
I have no need for parting, nor
Bruised hearts. I threw in my lot
With the apple
That you gave me.

Keelmen Heaving in Coals by Moonlight

after J.M.W. Turner

He's watching them loading the boats on Tyneside.
His heart is agitated – how fast they work.
The nightly loading of boats along the bank,
Lit by flame and gas, departing and returning
Higher and lighter in the water and then loaded again.
Although his heart is merely a pump made of chambers,
An automatic muscle, clenching and releasing the blood
Speeding it on to be oxygenated, returning it spent,
He feels it holds some emotion in its sinew,
Some memory in the constant, working ventricles.
He has no time. The river is fast, the keelmen
Work and work. Well he knows how the landscape
Changes, declines and dies, the composition is lost –
Or worse still, held and pocketed like a stone.
All he can do is paint his heart's blood into the ochre
And his blank passion into the sky's arc.

Puberty

after Edvard Munch

Lying face down on the pier
She can see the starfish, layered
Sometimes three deep. She lifts one
In her net, a delicate purple, turns
The net in the water and watches it fall.

It lands upside down and rights itself
Slowly, arduously, curling limbs up
One by one until the weight overturns it
And the little tentacles latch it back to the shells.
She watches the motion, belly-down on the wood.

The party has begun at the house. Lanterns flicker
Under the awning and they are clapping a speech,
So she stands and hooks the net over her shoulder
Walks back slowly; the net is dripping on the path
And the guests are clapping louder and louder.

Later she is rolling a flag in the darkness
Rolling and rolling it between her long fingers
To find the perfect smoothness, and a man touches
Her waist. He says he saw her fishing, asks her
What she caught. Nothing at all. The flag uncurls.

He will take her fishing, he says. Downwater
The fish are plump and constant, he has a boat.
And he comes briefly too close, please go.
After that she watches him from outside.
He moves around, he invites, he smiles.

Song of a Wanderer

I am fearless. Fearlessness was seeded in me
In a small flat where all the talk was children's babble
And soft spider replies: *doggie, choochoo, baba*
And the kitchen clattered and shook with gravy
Boiling over. The bread rose
The meat bubbled in the heat, and crooked spiderfingers
Laid the pastry ring across the seething curd.
I was fearless with wanting to dress my own small body
Walk with long, straight legs down to the street
Before the vegetables, ready mashed and served,
Before the napkin, tucked into my skirt.

But wherever I go I find the same sweet harem
Cloysome to my heart. The same old women and the babies
The same babble. I taste the same smell of meat
From high-up windows. I watch the same old fingers
Kneading bread and see the ancient ring mark on the crust.
And when they ask me, 'Why not have a rest?' on some bed
So high and soft and melting, I say, 'Yes. I'm really very tired.'
And unroll, in a headache of a dream, my limbs
So weary from their walking. Yes, I am captive
To the piecrust and the stove, the women and their talking,
The children's little grip.

Aquarium

The children are at the aquarium.
The dark tanks are filled with their reflections
Gazing eyes, little lips, fumbling
And knuckles wandering where the water ends.

The piranha fish have mumbling mouths
On each side they sparkle with gold glitter
Broken-nosed, flattish, ominous, they
Ignore the painted skeleton, pirate clutter.

And catfish, broad and ancient-whiskered
Swim closer to the glass and freeze
Gnarled like hundred-year-old trees
Felled and used for battering rams in sieges.

But in the conger eels' tank I see
The thick sinew of their hate
Disappear into the dank depressing weed
As slowly as the meditating snake.

And crabs tap at the glass and call us over
To poke the sticky anemones and maul
The mermaid's purses lying in the shallows
And stroke their velvet backs and hold their claws.

The nautilus pompilus tank is empty
But at the very back and caught in weed
The tiniest little sac of slippery matter
It looks much like an embryo enwombed.

We press closer. The little thing is pulsing
And transparent – manifest and lonely.
Beneath it, rubbish collected from a beach:
A bottle and a rope, unwinding slowly.

Maternity

The maternity ward has a sleepless pallor
This hour of the morning, a womb-warmth.
Here we are with our trolley in the day room
And it is barely day. The very first.
Still black outside, the radio is playing
Quietly to night workers resisting sleep
On their way home. We are alone. Bewildered.
Floating in a time before time:
Zero hour, zero day
Never again will we be this close
To the starting line, the beginning of it all.
It makes me sad, to set the clock as sure as this
To hold tight in my arms a measure of my own life
And watch the mists rising in the gloom,
Tears are rolling down the gown.
Hormones, they tell me.
The chemicals leaving my born-again blood.
The night draining from my born-again body.
Get used to the morning, little light.
We are separate and alive, you and I,
Picking out tunes quietly resistant
To sleep and dream.

Lot's Wife

I put everything into a grain sack
And fled. Because we are righteous, he said.

But oh, I would have preferred to be beautiful.

I took nothing but food. The children's toys
And nothing for me, although two novels

Lay trembling in the fire's heat. Take me. Choose me.
In case of fire take care, I read,

But care is the heaviest of all.

After the wind came the earthquake
And fire and then the still small voice
Brushed us along the streets and we ran

The lonely streets where the dung and decay
Would come sure as a flood and a furnace.
And women's faces will melt, he said

And he will take back the bone he once lent
He said. But the breast is now closed.

Still you are the righteous. I am not.
We have never climbed like this in our lives
The scenic spots and the coin telescopes
Are hours behind. I will do something bad

Wrung out in this way, in the wild
With the roots showing sharp
And the bags, and the nails.
I would prefer to be them.
No longer of him.

Take back the bone and throw it
So it arches and spins through the air
And is seized by wild dogs

Who sleep in the day and are kicked
Lying with their sixteen nipples exposed
In underground passes.

But in darkness and now their black lips are drawn
And their wolf teeth are white. Toss them
That bone.

The city was built on a grid and at night
From planes it appeared a luminous cage
I did not dance, it is true.

I covered my head. I threw coins
To the poor and spooned soup
Into bowls, and touched shoulders and smiled.

I washed their hands.
But I could have been sheer and cool
And worn feathers and gold
There is not much difference. I was not allowed.

What have I got within me that is righteous?
Only the love of a people on the brink
Of disaster. The kindness of those
Who will die stinking

Between paper walls.
No. I envy the ones
Who did as they chose –

You'd say depraved. As I climb
All alone and into the wilderness
With a Lord and a box of matches

And the universe expanding
Speckled with stars racing apart
Lighting me with their ancient destruction

Your mineral words dissolve
Into the ground from whence they came
And the small voice is gone.

Look at your people.
I speak for the first time. Look
At your own life.

And so I turn. I turn
And I see –

Motherlove

Her wreathed face is golden. The gold of the light
In the wood, dividing the bluebells two ways,

His is the watchful soft light: twilight
The dog is brought in and the child looks out hard –

Where the light stops, the world stops.
He has already asked, will they die too?

I say, never. Never. Wrong to lie
But see her, chattering, singing

Pecking like a bluetit at her many toys,
Or him, sweet and straight and dusk-pale –

It is not a lie. I will not allow it.

Pleiades

Look hard and the image is too clumsy
To bear scrutiny – look away and you should
Glimpse it from the corner of your eye. Gaze often
At Mars and you will see your quiet childhood
Reluctant childhood, idyll from here,
Six slight stars, grinning with raised thumbs
At the long-forgotten perceiver and now at you
The seventh has passed beyond the range of human view.

Carnation, Bible

Flower of your mother's eye
When you first took flowers from him:
Little bespectacled man who bowed
And offered violets to your simpering
And his hand to your hand. Temptation
And the flower was a dry carnation
Folded in a Bible and it snapped
From its pale stalk as you tripped
Through the factory one last time, O Eve,
He said, O submissive one, walk with me
In my worker's paradise, in your heeled shoes
And smartest coat, let me lead you
To the door of my heart, peer round it, Eve
All flour to the elbows, aproned, unsleeved,
Beckon me in for pie and love
And slap and tickle. And the children we have
We will instruct in Bible ways and temple,
And temperance and temper, temper.
And the flower dries flat between leaves of the Bible
And the serpent weeps, but goes unheeded
In the terrible mornings, the stuck-pig-screaming
Of the littlest ones, her Cain and Abel.

Dinosaurs

I am reading a book about dinosaurs.
The time devours us, my son and me
As we learn the origins of jaws
And the closure of the Uralian Sea.

Regard the landscape, trilobites.
Is it not fine, all grass and skies
And uninhabited by humankind
As the artist exemplifies.

Several hundred million years
Will pass and guiltless waste away
With the fruit upon the trees
With the load of day on day.

The earth has never lived so lush
Has never spawned so many lives
Still we would perish in this glut
Amongst the earliest crocodiles

And never learn to live beyond
The constrictions of our little time
Or see the developing cynodonts
As more than torment to the mind

Unmanned, the Mesozoic comes
I lie uncurled upon the sand
About me stand the gymnosperms
I'm praying for a certain end

Warning

O burghers and solid citizens!
Take heed! Remember walking out in heels
Barelegged, thin-shouldered in the river air,
Remember throwing cans, remember
The delayed clatter above the precinct.
Remember not needing food,
Not wanting anything, squatting in the weeds
And watching night end. Be dismayed, gentlemen
When you see yourself in the lift's mirror –
Be dismayed that time has passed and time
Is cruel. Silent couples doing the crossword
At different ends of the table, remember when
You caught each other's eye and were dumb
As lambs and as foolish. Remember that?
Make an effort and dig deep
Inside yourselves, put down the bags,
The fan of cards and open-mouthed, blushing
Make that involuntary gesture with the arm
When a shameful moment trespasses on our
Ordered lives.

Hope

When I was young a fever took me
And the doctor said it was no good
So they christened me in bed and called me Hope.

I chose one road from those that lay before me.
I lived, and watched the days and then the months
Take me further from the death that must have claimed me.

And soon that moment lay bundled in passed time.
Still later I chose the right hand of my Grandpa,
His fist clutched nothing, the sweet was in the left.

They say my disappointment made him cry.
The first tears of his illness, I saw his eyes
Were wheels of blue. He unwrapped the sweet.

I sat on the kerb till night and watched the games,
Choosing not to play and not to fight. Nor
To stay there – those children who are now

All grown up and still at home. I chose to look away.
They kicked me. I chose not to reply, but limped
Inside with bitter pride traced right through me.

Then the boys and then the men I kept myself from –
Each one revealed a well-lit street of life
A taxi, bicycle ride from here –

A journey I did not deign to plan.
(The arrogance was mine.) Until I chose to fall in love
And follow someone else's fate.

Still when I feel the weight of choices made
Upon me, in the branching of the trees
And maps of foreign places

I take the car and drive it through the lanes
And when I reach a fork I stop and think
And easing off the brake, I choose and hope.

Guests

A jay falls across the road and then rises
As we speed away. Past the King's Arms
A man on a bike, a pie shop and a family-owned
Funeral parlour and monumental masons.

And Grandma sits, monumental herself,
Pursed and upright and looking forward
Displaying no trace of human thought
As if carved from limestone on a beach.

We have been driving her round. Departing
Guest, we show her the very best of the land
To take with her. She reminds us of the presence
Of other lands, other existences and planets.

Reaching this village for tea she makes talk
In a language she is rapidly forgetting
Amongst the foreign ritual of a teashop,
The aluminium pot, the strainer, the spoon.

And then the graveyard. We study it,
Just short of the weeded canal, the closed station,
And swollen with the waiting crowds
Of a once important town.

A transit town, full of travellers to the ports
Who took the trains, the barges, the stagecoaches
And left in their droves. Here they are:
Standing military fashion amongst the willow trees.

We hurry away back to the waiting car,
Arm in arm like visitors to a city stumbling
On a station midway through the holiday,
A reminder of the shortness of it all.

Back past the village shop, pub and funeral parlour
In the sudden dusk. A jay rising and falling.
I look at it, gape, see it again, as if
I were the stranger here.

Does dust speak to dust
She enquires, dark
With the words, the effort
Of voicing a sudden lack

Of faith, of hope? Hopelessness.

And there it was, like a skull
Wrapped in cloth and cloves
In a trunk of clothes. Her faith

Crumbling like old paper unfolded.
And all that day she had busied herself
Breathless. Setting her house in order

Like a woman with child. Opening case
After case and offering jewels –
Pearls would look lovely against your
Pale skin, my darling –
Scarves and pins.

Holding the baby. So much the woman
The mother and lover. I wore this once,
At a party, you know. I was
Admired.

And now this: a sudden stare
Into the radiant sun of it –
The endless opening and closing
Of days without her,
Nights without her.

Will I be with him? I don't think so.
There will be nothing,
Wouldn't you say?

I betray her with cheap comforts.
I betray her with lowered eyes.
I betray her with youth.

I fit the noose of pearls that night
Over my head. I lay them, knotted and
Looped on my breastplate
I make love in her pearls.

No. Dust is silent.

The Ring

At our last meeting she gave me her ring.
A Victorian ring, passed from an aunt
To a sister, through channels and eddies
Of friends and relations until now:
Washed up on a bank made steep by meandering.

No more leaping through streams.
No more damselfly catching.

And the cut is Victorian, says the jeweller,
Refitting the ring to my own ring-finger.
The turquoises, smooth like pebbles to jump to.
The diamonds glistening like water to run through.
I wear it although it is too brilliant for me.

It is the ribbon-like skim of the bream,
The kingfisher's turquoise sloping and sinking,
The water cutting in angles over the branches.

Touched with a quaint and languorous elegance,
A day of reclining and drawing and stitching.
In this ring I should brush the thick hair past my shoulders
And not wash vegetables, and refrain from writing –
Only albums, notelets, inscriptions on flyleaves.

No more leaping through streams.
No more damselfly catching.

Two days ago Autumn arrived.
I was sitting at the window chewing a pencil
And Autumn came. Stopped and put down belongings
Sniffed the air like a sharp-nosed dog
Worried the overloaded nettle with its toe.
And from then on there was chill in the morning
And birds clattered in the branches and collected
And although the day was warm and even hot
And everyone laughed at me with my Autumn
And even I wondered if I had not been mistaken,
Some withering had begun, and a tarnishing
And a scalding of the air and the earth
And I was proud, proud, that I had
Known its shape, with all my superfluity
And unnecessary fluster, I had still sniffed it out,
What good it did me.

The Coat

Natural ends are odd-even with beginnings.
Today I felt the incoming of spring
As we parted, each clutching winnings

To blow on the ordinary humdrum things
Stooped like the man whose coat
Was ripped from him not by the wind

But by the sun, who warming, gloats;
So the world slips off cloak and lock and seal
Flutters a thousand pale banknotes.

Yes, it is here. The air wears the feel,
The cut of spring, and winter slinks about
Tight-belted and down-at-heel.

Winter, I will see you out
The sun is rising over hill and fable
And placing gentle fingers on my coat

Prizes it from me, as he alone is able.

Butcher's Wood

The very last harebell and a flower that bears a scurrilous name
Round here, and pinkish yew berries and the great yellow hands
Of leaves palm-down to the needled floor. All of it dull compost
Away from here, better un-pocketed and watched, better left alone

For poachers' ghosts and their transparent sacks. The painless traps
That rabbits skip through, the painless axes jointing painless game.
They are so very slight and clever, these poaching ghosts, dodging
Keeper, master and the master's men, who have flogged a ghost
                                                      not once –

Painlessly – for picking harebells and carrying them away.
And this is where the priest must hide. Finger to cursed lip, knelt
Behind a pyre of rotten logs, too much like fate to be close observed
But not blind to the black-lipped snails and spiders – praise him!

Praise him who has created Butcher's Wood! An end to heresy on
                                                      this Isle!
And there is a woodlark, and there a greenfinch, so late this year
And so calm, although they should be safely hid by now.
Turn your mind to your Lord, man. Bird and spider cannot save
                                                      you now.

But how to bear death in Butcher's Wood? Fleshly jointed like a crow
In harder times, blackly shaken over snow, trapped and gutted –
How? And if faith hibernates like a slick vole? Faith-mouse's
Shrinking patter, Father, send me word. Send me word in
                                                      Butcher's Wood.

Quiet. Another ghostly poacher trudges past. The harebell trembles
Courage, harebell. Now the Lord will send a sign. Hazel wavers
Bee hovers. And quiet once again. Can that be all, Lord? This haven?
Is this your petty pity, Lord? Man sinks down on leaf hands, prays.

The voice of my beloved
It came to me of an evening
Of an evening it came to me
And said hurry up. Hurry

It said to me, and I was out
Smelling the roses, just watching
And having fun and the blackbirds
Were as black as death,

Hurry up said that voice, and
I was out there folding washing
And smelling the roses, watching
How dew lay miles deep on the clothes

And the roses smelt so rosy and
The blackbirds slept and sang
As black as seed, as sharp as thorn
I heard my loved one's voice that evening

See the blackness on the hillside
Hurry hurry drop the clothes
Having fun smelling roses!
Hurry hurry, said my loved one

The Quartet

The quartet are going home
With their instruments on their backs
Pausing to lock the room where they pass
So many hours, string, bow and wand
Alive and hovering over the wood. At last!
Coax it, just a little louder. It comes.

The bus ride, they make mild conversation
Outer life the simple echo of the tune
And one hums. Tomorrow we meet again
They think. Tomorrow we start anew
On the second part. Fingering it through
Quick with a calm, subtle elation.

But this is as lonely as the diver whose fingers are lost
From view. This is as lonely as the mountaineer
Whose handhold is coming loose, as lonely as the mother
Behind the pram on a bitter afternoon. Some days there is only
The boy in my mind, alone at night on a sacred island
Clutching a golden cup beneath his coat.

Green Man

Green man, does it pain you, the ever-issuing
Greenness from your mouth, does it choke you?
Is it a curse you long to bite free from?
A vine-cord to be knotted and left to wither.
Wouldn't you like to feel where skin ends,
Leaves begin? Where the fragrant hawthorn grows alone
And is picked by lovers, debating on pricked fingers
Its scent. Wouldn't you like to lay your foliose head in a lap?

Or are you keeper of our light souls: always on the midpoint
Half-human, half-plant, flitting out and in,
Unable to rest and forever suffering with the constant
Shifting growth. The yew sends its roots to claim us in death,
But you watch us passing through the many gates and many houses
We are pleased to call our lives.